EL MIRAGE
IMPRESSIONS

Iconografix
PO Box 446
Hudson, Wisconsin 54016 USA

Library of Congress Card Number: 2001132805

ISBN 1-58388-059-3

01 02 03 04 05 06 07 5 4 3 2 1

Book Proposals

Iconografix is a publishing company specializing in books for transportation enthusiasts. We publish in a number of different areas, including Automobiles, Auto Racing, Buses, Construction Equipment, Emergency Equipment, Farming Equipment, Railroads & Trucks. The Iconografix imprint is constantly growing and expanding into new subject areas.

Authors, editors, and knowledgeable enthusiasts in the field of transportation history are invited to contact the Editorial Department at Iconografix, Inc., PO Box 446, Hudson, WI 54016.

EL MIRAGE

I M P R E S S I O N S

PHOTOGRAPHIC
AND
WRITTEN
ESSAYS

by M. de Lesseps

and friends
with a preface by Earl Wooden

Special thanks to the Southern California Timing Association for permission to use the results which appear here.

Designed by Scott Vile and Nathan Sanborn in Stone Sans and Dante at the Ascensius Press, Portland, Maine.

PREFACE

RUNNING THE DIRT

*Land Speed Racing on California's
El Mirage Dry Lake*

Why the heck do we do that Dry Lake Racing thing? Race weekend is usually very hot, or sometimes very cold (this is the Mojave Desert), windy, dirty and very noisy. A very long way from golf, card game, or couch potato TV.

Land Speed Racing time trials is an attempt by non-professional, unsponsored sportsmen to do a feat that is extremely complex, time consuming, expensive and sometimes dangerous.

And therein lies the reward, over-coming a challenge of rather Herculean proportions. Any man that is drawn to motor sports may try to participate. It is "Everyman's sport."

I believe most men in their work or sport need a challenge with (if successfully accomplished) its proportionate psychological rewards, to feel fulfilled as a man. That's the real reason men will go to war if asked, accept tough mental/physical assignments at work and try to care for and raise a family. We have a few great women participating at the chassis / engine builder level, but more often as a driver. But it is more often a male thing. Maybe it's the testosterone.

The suggestion of building a race car and high performance engine essentially from scratch is daunting to say the least. With enough tenacity, we run up the learning curve as fast as we can, get a ton of help from friends and professionals, throw a bucket of money at it, think about it most waking hours, and somehow it comes to fruition.

The effort to pull this off has everything to do with the resulting thrill of driving and enormous satisfaction of breaking a Land Speed Record.

It is the totality of the effort it took to get there and do what no man has done before, that is the thrill: the satisfaction of a job well done. The leaving of your mark, at least for a moment in time.

The feeling is not egotism as some would say (especially spouses after you've spent the new washer / dryer money on race car tires), but rather a unique and very personal feeling of accomplishment that no one can really share with you.

Contrary to popular belief it is not a daredevil sport where one pushes the limits and risk to almost sure disaster. It is a complex and carefully calculated challenge.

Land Speed Racing is very much a group sport, very much a sport of fellowship and friendship. But also of a peculiar aloneness, truly a sport of individual passion.

If you are destined to be bitten by the addictive racing bug, what that bug screams at you is . . . can you do this?

EARL WOODEN
Member, Southern California Timing Association; Bonneville Nationals, Inc.

RACE MORNING

El Mirage Dry Lake, California

Dawn of race day at the "Lakes." Barely light, quiet, cool. Majority of the one thousand camped out on the lake bed in motor homes, trailers, and trucks are still asleep.

From the moment you wake you are very focused on the time. It's 6:00 AM, and you have ninety minutes to prepare your race car and get to the starting line up. Drivers meeting is 7:30 AM.

You have slept off the lake bed because though your Timing Association has a permit for the race on Sunday, El Mirage is an open Federal Recreation area. Most people on the lake bed will not drive a race vehicle Sunday morning, so their focus is more on partying Saturday night. The outsiders, and some of our own, race around on motorbikes and dune buggy's late into the night, oblivious to others need for sleep. You know that if you drive a race car with little or no sleep mistakes happen. That could be catastrophic.

As an owner/crew chief/driver your mind set is different than the carefree spectator. More of a loner, continuously focused on everything that must be done and the remaining time left to do it. It's your responsibility, no one else can do it.

In the days prior to race weekend you prepped the race car, loaded it on it's trailer, loaded the truck with most of the shop, and on Saturday morning towed to El Mirage.

Saturday was spent setting up your pit area, getting the car inspected. The engine fired, to again check for problems.

On race morning the feelings and attitude are one of determination, pride in your race car, anticipation of setting a land speed record, and a bit of nerves. In a little while you'll be going across El Mirage Dry Lake at 250 mph.

Arriving at your pit, your partner is there, ready to go to work. Fire up the generator. Oil and water is heated, tire pressure is checked. Fuel in, car cleaned up. 7:00 AM., light the engine. Good long warm-up. Car is on blocks, run through the gears, warming transmission and rear end. Change to race spark plugs, check and re-check everything. Button it up and head for the starting line.

Things went smooth. Your crew, like you, is totally focused. It's not always like this. Takes a special commitment to take this serious enough. With two people we accomplish what race teams many times our size do in other forms of motor sports.

Race car is in lineup, go to drivers meeting. Patrols are out, track is ready, it's show time.

Your helmet, jacket, gloves are on top of the race car. You slip into driving pants and boots. The routine of getting you dressed, into the car and belted up is rehearsed. No mistakes needed now.

Parachutes, fire systems are armed. Switches turned on. Starter checks your belts and the door is closed. You're ready!

The starter motions "You're up." Fire the engine, look down the track to see if dust has cleared from previous runner, so you can see where you're going. Your partner is waiting for your thumbs up signal that "it's a go." You give it. The starter signals Go, you feel the push truck moving you. The track is yours.

You've got about thirty seconds to try and get your record. All the preparation comes down to this moment. Focus! Focus! Focus!

Pop the Jerico four speed stick into low, rap the engine, engage and launch. Lack of traction is the enemy. Give it all the power you can in low gear without getting totally sidewise. Work the throttle, engine screaming, tires slipping, shift at 8,000 rpm. Push clutch in, lift momentarily, hit the shift lever hard. Second gear, better traction, feather it a little as rear end of car is coming around. Shift into third, enough speed and down force now to flat foot it.

Totally focused on track location. Stay between the cones. Shift into fourth, engine sounds good. Finish line, timing traps coming up. Look at tachometer. Where tach comes up to in fourth gear determines whether you made it. Looks good. Hand goes up to chute lever. As soon as you clear lights pull chute handle and push in clutch. You're coasting now at 250 mph. When you feel the chute hit, push fuel shut off, kill magneto, and move shift lever to neutral.

You're moving at 100 yards per second. Any chute problem, pull backup chute. Return two hands to wheel. Still moving very fast, don't lose concentration. Stay on track till speed drops to about fifty mph, down almost a mile into shut off area. Arc off left, stop at return road. Unbuckle, get out, nice deep breath, ask nearest patrol or spectator how fast?

Driver Assumptions:

1. Totally focused during entire run, ignore all distractions including fear. No time.

2. Total trust in car mechanically, not the time to worry about those things.

3. Total focus on maximizing speed of car in all gears without losing it. It is a race on the dirt against the clock.

4. Trust that no spectator will cross the track in front of you, couldn't miss them anyway.

5. Enjoy the ride, record or not, you've challenged yourself and won.

6. Enjoy the rest of the morning, talk the run over, brag a little with anyone who will listen.

EARL WOODEN

Earl Wooden, born in Hollywood, California in 1931 became involved in the early Southern California Hot Rod scene in the 1940's. Earl owned and raced a variety of roadsters and coupes on the Dry Lakes and Bonneville Salt Flats during these years. In 1955 Earl took a 36-year hiatus from racing, returning in 1991. After climbing a very steep learning curve returning to land Speed racing . . . it is now his retirement hobby.

In 1998 Earl Wooden and his Crosley were inducted into the Dry Lakes Racing Hall of Fame.

Some of the many friends who have helped with the cars success include Ron Benham, Leonard Carr, Ron Shaver, Jay Steel, and Ken Walkey.

2   THE PAST

In the late '20s and '30s, the idea that an automobile could be tinkered with or modified to get a little more speed became very popular, much to the annoyance of the authorities. The tinkerers and modifiers were successful. Speeds were growing at an alarming rate. As this popular endeavor grew the fears of the public grew with it. Street racing was dangerous. A better venue had to be found.

As a result, the interested parties organized clubs which arranged time trials on several high desert dry lakes in California. These clubs eventually came together as the Southern California Timing Association. The S.C.T.A., as it became known, managed meets with marked courses and timing equipment run by volunteers. The Dry Lakes were huge, wide open, inhospitable spaces where a car could be run flat out with relative safety.

Some very smart people have been going to the flats to try their ideas for a long, long time. It stands to reason that almost everything has been tried more than once, yet within the confines of this kind of competition (often against their own record) improvements in performance are found resulting in new records. Also appealing is a certain stubborn regard for a thing that works. No matter how archaic it might seem, there is no reason to reinvent it.
It stays the same.

Sixty years later people are still at it, highly organized and still chasing speed. The influence of these racers on the overall development of the automobile is enormous.

We owe them a note of thanks.

3 RATIONALE

Since this is a book of photographs something needs to be said about the making of pictures. I have always been interested in early dry lakes cars as they were the original hot rods and I have worked in and around photography all my professional life.

The decision to make my way out to El Mirage, California to work on an essay covering the Dry Lake activities in photographs came easily, getting there and putting it into a body of work has taken considerably longer. I believe this is more than just another book of car pictures, and even for those interested in photography perhaps something more than the usual film, ASA, lens and technical drill normally found on this subject today; a different way of thinking.

This project was to have been photographed on one weekend in July. Just what could be covered on Saturday and Sunday. Something personal, a

statement about the people and the cars who make this what it is.

The site was open and well lit. It was 110° in the shade. Flat, open space for miles and a tight nomadic community of trucks, vans, campers and trailers with machines all about. A crowd all intensely at their work, but if one needed something as simple as a washer, the nearest one was fifty miles away. Light and dark, shade and heat. Perfect photographic conditions.

A Point
of View

*A Minister . . . not liking the umpire's
call at the ball game shouts . . .
"Thou has eyes but thou seest not!"*

Here are some thoughts about photography. If you treat your picture taking as serious work it can be very rewarding. In this exploration we will try to get to a point beyond any of the mechanical or technical aspects of the craft. By the time you have worked at it long enough to feel competent, a decent sharp, well exposed negative should be a matter of fact, though even that (on occasion) can elude an experienced pro.

Before you release the shutter . . . that you need to SEE everything: composition, light, activity and the participation of the subjects even if the subject is inert, (unmoving) is critical. Choices, lots of them all tied to decisions that have to be made in an instant, determine the results of your venture.

It is a process. Most start with *how* they would like to go about the business of shooting a picture. Get the camera, collect the elements or participants and get it all organized. *How* is not the place to start even if you are working in a situation you can control. When you have a clear idea of *what* you are trying to accomplish the *how* will become a lot easier. You have a plan.

Point of view. Any situation offers opportunity to own it. Anyone can take a picture, but the quality of an "Owned Image" is difficult to achieve.

Walker Evans, a complex man, shot seemingly simple photographs. It was the kind of work that once seen was approachable but unexpected. Signage in the streets, everyday life woven seamlessly through time. People riding on the subway, portraits of fellow travelers never noticed by passers-by, but brought to life by vision, by insight. A close look at his life's work can reveal a sensitivity to more than a technically well produced image, more than portraits on a subway. Or signs. Walker Evans' point of view is an emotional language articulated with uncommon images.

Alexey Brodovitch, art director, *Harper's Bazaar*. Teacher, critic and observer, he was important to a change in how we see things, but he did it back in the thirties. His magazine spreads exploded with lush images seen only before as conservative adjuncts to the written word. Photography became dominant in his hands, he took the images brought to him by working photographers and added his point of view, powerful images run through the gutter and bleeding at all sides. No publication was ever the same once his work hit the stands and was seen. He was able to express his point of view and extend those of others with his inventive spirit. This point of view helped produce a new cultural reality.

These are only two examples, there are hundreds more, all with something to say and in very different ways. Having a look at the work of people who really did it all might help, but even if you study every photographic image ever made you will ultimately have to make some of your own. What is important is to develop a way of seeing uniquely on your own. It has everything to do with what you take a picture of and a lot to do with how you do it. You should work for a perceptive and emotional result. It's not the camera, lens or the film and really not even the subject, it's all about *what* you see first and then *how* you do it.

For example, if we made a situation where one could provide a model, a camera and a dozen participants not necessarily in the arts, to make portraits of the model, how many of that dozen would take the one remarkable shot? The memorable image that would have it all, originality, a point of view, everything.

Of that dozen how many do you think would make the "owned image"?

For a difference you might say, the model is better portrayed unsmiling as a smile changes the features, distorts the true image. What if Leonardo Da Vinci had asked Mona Lisa to lose the smile, would his portrait have stood the test of time? An expressionless portrait may show structure but does it show the real person? Portraits devoid of any emotion may be a good idea, but I can name at least one well known photographer who has made this his own though he may not have invented it. Look at the work of others: study it but always remember there is an honest world of difference between what you discover in the works of others and what you discover in your own.

When you set up to shoot an automobile, what do you see, what do you select, what makes a good image? The perfect view of the auto designers art? Some close-up view that one would normally not notice. A shadow cast by the car's defining shape? Interaction between human and machine? Something predictable? Should you capture something readily apparent or should you interpret? What? . . . is the question, what will it take to make an "owned image?" What indeed.

The point being, photography has been around a very long time and there is little that has not been tried. It is a great leveler, everyone seems to start at or near the same place, unlike drawing or painting, where the drawn or painted line has it's maker's mark. Should this suggest that you might not discover something? That you might not find a distinctive point of view? Not at all, just remember the most complex problems usually prove to be the most interesting. Finding your own point of view is the most difficult. Try reaching deep inside for that inner stimuli.

Having a point of view is one thing, having your own that is definable is another thing entirely. How does one do this? I would suggest that you make whatever effort it takes to develop and define your ability to "see" into a given situation. Work for an intellectual depth that will not settle for the easy way out and always asks the question, *What* am I doing? Am I looking at or into this situation or what is really offered, can I see some emotional language here (am I just styling and trending)?

Here is a very short list to illustrate what is meant by an owned image. At least one name in this list should recall an image that is recognizable even if you're not a student of art or photography. Ansel Adams, Norman Rockwell, Maxfield Parrish, Monet, Van Gogh, Picasso, Jackson Pollock and Mickey Mouse.

If you can't come up with any image within this list of names don't worry about it. The list is to show beyond the name of an artist how the image could be more memorable. If you work at it you too might find your way to an owned image.

Altering Images

You will see that all the images in this work have a small black border. The reason for this is to illustrate that none of the photographs in the essay have been cropped. They are all "as seen" through the view finder when shot. The black border is made by the film holder when the print is made as its opening is slightly larger than the exposed 35 mm film image on the negative. When I'm shooting I know that the pictures will not be cropped. This is important to me as part of the discipline of work.

For those of you curious about what I used for equipment, Black and White Kodak T Max film, an old Nikon F, no auto focus (I got it in the '60s) and one 28 mm lens to keep a constant, consistent look. All with the same pair of eyes so to speak.

Do I have a problem with cropping photographs? No, not at all. As an art director I'd say I have cropped my share of pictures, had my way with them but that

was hard commercial work where all the elements had a part to play in an overall piece.

I hope you enjoy the El Mirage images. They are what they are. You will decide whether there is a point of view.

The difficulties encountered by someone trying to make an "owned image" are much the same as those of racers pursuing a record. Each has only the past and some hard work to guide them.

When you look at the photographs you will notice that most of the participant's cars have a number visible. It may be of interest to see their results in the table following the photographs. The Southern California Timing Association does a great job of keeping track of each run. All done by the many volunteers from clubs that make up the S.C.T.A.

Note that land speed racing is not a spectator sport, no cheering crowds (on a run they could not be seen or heard anyway).

4 THE HOT ROD CONNECTION

When I returned to the East from my travels, I had some discussions with friends who know El Mirage and share my interest in Hot Rods. I found two who, though they are not writers by trade, were willing to express themselves on this subject (because they couldn't do otherwise) given the opportunity.

I am grateful that they did because I think they say it best. You can judge.

They both appear here, with their current Hot Rod projects. My thanks to both Pete Smythe and Sam Samson.

TWO ESSAYS ON HOT RODDING

by

Pete Smythe

&

Sam Samson

Pete Smythe's Ride. Here is Pete and his reconstruction of the Model A coupe that started it all for him. It actually contains parts, front axle, hairpins and frame sections from the original car.

Wide Whites and Moon Caps

by Pete Smythe

To a twelve year old kid growing up in Augusta, Maine in the mid-fifties, California might as well have been a myth. That is, until a hot summer Sunday afternoon when all the definitions changed.

A rumored phenomenon known as hot rodding became reality in the form of a chopped, channeled (hard), fenderless Model A coupe being towed up Green Street in a futile attempt to get the tri-carbed flathead to fire. Hanging on the edge of the cluster of "big guys," I soaked up discussions of spark advance, fuel pressure, and other esoteric engine terminology (along with some new expletives!) This was heady stuff!

The car disappeared, still on the end of the tow chain, but a fire was sparked in the eyes of a flattopped kid. A fire that is still fueled by that chance encounter more than forty years ago.

The coupe was a vision in proportion, stance, and attitude. But particularly striking were the whitewalls and Moon caps. I wasn't sure why those features hit me the way they did, but the sun glinting off those spun aluminum discs was, for this kid, an epiphany.

Spare quarters were not easy to come by in those days, but when an odd job or bottle collecting paid off, the change was quickly exchanged for pocket-size car magazines—*Rod & Custom* preferred. From these resources, the basis of my infatuation became apparent, and the dry lakes coupes—chopped, channeled, fenderless, with (gasp) Moon discs, put things in perspective.

Bonneville, Muroc, and El Mirage became real places (but still about as accessible from Green Street as the moon). Names like Winfield, Xydias, Thompson, Navarro, and Edelbrock became bigger than life, and cars

that graced those dog-eared pages—the Chrisman Bros. coupe, the SoCal coupe, and numerous hi-boy deuce roadsters—molded and sculpted this passion that could only be sated by total immersion.

In Maine, the closest thing to dry lakes racing is called a "mud run," and gives a whole different definition to "total immersion." But hot-rodding's second generation mutation, drag racing, could be found only *half* a world away—Sanford, Maine. *Maine!!* We were part of the real world after all! Thus, this fickle flattop

head was turned from salt to asphalt, and
a certain chopped, channeled (hard),
fenderless Model A coupe, with a now
wailing flathead and C/Comp shoe-
shined white in the quarter window,
reaffirmed the definition of Hot Rod in
the kid's vision, and the Moon discs added
the exclamation point! (Only now, I knew
why they were screwed on.)

PETE SMYTHE
Standish, Maine

Sam Samson, by his own definition, "The Original Hot Rod Junkie" at work on his Bonneville coupe. Not shown, his '34 coupe "She Bad," a well-known Hot Rod.

Sam Samson's Comments

In a recent conversation with Mike "DeVillbliss" deLesseps, the subject of El Mirage came up. Mike had recently completed his third round trip from Maine to California and back in the Chevy powered, '40 Ford Tudor. His trip included the Mecca of Hot Rods, El Mirage, Bonneville too.

While we discussed El Mirage we wondered why some are still attracted to El Mirage or Bonneville for that matter. In this age of Nascar, national rod runs, cross country cruises, some guys are still out there racing at these Meccas, relatively unknown, without sponsors, in their home-built Hot Rods. That's the way they want it though. If these places ever commercialized there most certainly would be a drastic change. Hot Rodders have been racing at the Meccas since the twenties and things really haven't changed that much. The bottom line of the entry sheet reads something like this: At the end of the season, if your car is the points champ, to whom do we mail the trophy? No money, no endorsements, just a handshake and "See ya next year."

Now I must admit anything and everything I know about Hot Rods I learned through reading *Hot Rod*, *Rod 'n Custom*, *Car Craft*, etc. I started in the mid-fifties.

I presently own a '34 5-window, "SHE BAD," and I'm in the middle of my latest project, a chopped, '34 3-window, 351 Ford powered, being built for Bonneville—to be run in the Competition Coupe Class.

During a recent visit to my garage by some of my best friends—Hot Rodders, drag racers, street rod builders all, I found myself almost apologizing as to why I was building my latest project in the manner that I was. No fenders, radical chop, frame "Zeed" front and rear, louvers (they're not just on there for cosmetics ya know), belly pans, Moon

discs, "steelies" not "mags." I might even keep the straight axle.

In this day of "aerodynamically correct" Camaros and Firebirds, why would a guy want to build a 500 hp barn door! In my case, it all leads back to El Mirage, the pictures of the Hot Rods I saw in those magazines forty plus years ago. I want to run the way the legends did it. Chrismans, Piersons, Morimotos, Bob Rufi, Karl and Veda Orr, Harry Oka, and on and on. Even then I don't know if I'll go any faster than they did; who cares?

I once met Bob Pierson, the first thing he did was offer me a beer! He'd been readin' my mail. Then he showed me his photo album, all black and whites. The first ever car show, Muroc, El Mirage, Bonneville, street driven Hot Rods, pictures of Hot Rodders and on and on. He told me of when coupes were first allowed to race—before, only roadsters could race. He proceeded to tell me that

Bob, his brother Dick, and their friend (I believe his name was Dick Northrup), took the brothers' '36 coupe and put it in Northrup Aviation's wind tunnel and proceeded to chop it accordingly.

The Pierson brothers then took the coupe to El Mirage, I believe, and broke the existing (roadster) record by at least twenty miles an hour. Bob told me "What the other guys weren't familiar with was aerodynamics."

Their '34 3-window coupe was yet to be built. Aerodynamics—even back to the days of Harper's Rosamond, etc., the first thing the Hot Rodders did, after driving their cars to the race location, was take off the fenders, bumpers, lights, windshield, horns, anything that wasn't essential, to go fast.

Later on they chopped the tops, channeled the bodies, installed dropped axles, Moon discs, shaved door handles. Aerodynamics! That's why they did it. Louvers let the air in and got it out. Belly pans—streamlining—lean that windshield back further!

Quick changes—we raced El Mirage this weekend, next month it's a longer course—Bonneville. Skinny tires, less wind resistance, get that sucker down as low as you can get it. Let's put that motor back as far as we can for the maximum weight distribution.

That's what these Hot Rods are all about. That's why street rods look the way the do today, although I bet

most street rodders don't really know the reasoning behind it. El Mirage, Muroc, Bonneville, that's where it all started—that and the streets of Southern California.

That's the reason I build cars the way I do. I'm not into street machines—Camaros, Firebirds, etc. I'm into Hot Rods, thanks to the legends of Hot Rodding and the Meccas they drove to and "run what they brung."

I've been to Muroc, hope to go again. Someday, just maybe I'll race my car, pure Hot Rod, at Bonneville. I've never been to El Mirage—in my mind, I'm there every day, have been for over forty years. Maybe someday I'll get there. I talked to Frank Morimoto at Muroc, he showed me timing plaques dating back to the mid-thirties. But that's another story.

El Mirage, Muroc, Bonneville, the Bean Bandits, Pierson brothers, Xydias, and on and on again. That's why they call me "The Original Hot Rod Junkie." That's why I run an F.T.F.* plaque. Whenever I see a Hot Rod I think of these legends and wherever they raced. It's in my blood and I can't get it out! F.T.F.! Hot Rods forever.

Fordingly yours,
    Sam, T.O.H.R.J.

SAM SAMSON
Strong, Maine

* Forget the fenders

5 EL MIRAGE
PHOTOGRAPHIC ESSAY

96 Images Shot On the Dry Lake

July 16 and 17, 1995

Southern California, a little north of Adelento, Highway 395, on the high desert.
Bureau of Land Management site labeled: "Off-Highway Vehicle Recreation Area."

Getting a little closer, hints of the Dry Lake in the distance.

El Mirage Dry Lake, the little Ultra-Lite gives a sense of scale.

The Dry Lake surface, when it rains it turns to mud and is then baked by
the relentless desert sun back to a hard and flat surface.

Early morning arrivals on line to sign in.

No. 26. Tom's Muffler & Deming (Rod Riders). A very traditional '34 Ford 5W coupe.
Note split wishbone, dropped axle and radically chopped top.

No. 26. Smooth track style nose, painted on grille and flowing hood.

No. 26. Blown Flathead engine with homemade heads.
High-tech catch can all the way from the Orient.

No. 26. Tech Inspection to ensure driver safety.

No. 28. Another Tom's Muffler & Deming entry (Rod Riders).
Interesting angle on a Deuce Roadster.

No. 28. Quick Change Rear for easy rear axle gear ratio changes.
A great place for an Auto Parts sign.

No. 28. Here is just about everything one might expect to find in a
well turned out traditional Dry Lakes Racer.

No. 96. Scotty's Muffler (Sidewinders). Scotty told me this roadster was originally a coupe, altered to make it more competitive.

No. 96. In that same conversation Scotty said the car was nothing special, stock
frame, straight axles, big block, but it did go 243 MPH at El Mirage years ago.

No. 64. Kelly & Hall (Eliminators). The smoothest '34 Roadster ever.

No. 64. The view of the rear is as clean and smooth as the front.

No. 64. Tough Roll cage for a well-protected driver.

No. 64. Flathead powered, Kong heads, fuel injected and done right.

No number here. Big inline six, brings a smile as I recall back in the '50s it was an inline six that beat me every time at the drags. This is what they look like after a run or two down the Lake.

No. 185. John Bjorkman (Gear Grinders). Front body panel removed
for inspection. Note placement of tank in nose.

No. 185. Safety inspection. It was interesting to learn that many cars carry extra weight, a balance of ballast to help trim and traction.

No. 911. Fairly Honest Racing (Eliminators). The name reminds me of a
remark made by a competitor, "You must be cheating, because I'm
cheating, and you are beating me!"

No. 911. From the back end it looked like a traditional roadster, from here it looks like a good deal more. It ran 187.455 MPH on race day.

Window seen at El Mirage, might as well tell the world.

No. 150. McCain & Houtz (Super Fours).
A Pinto, slightly altered, a blown Flathead altered as well.

No. 150. A closer look at the injected, Mooneyham blown flat motor,
heads by Kong.

No. 150. Ed Houtz giving things a last lookover.

No. 150. Interior view, tach and oil pressure, what more does one need?

No. 150. No generation gap here, family values are strong.

No. 334. Clem Hiltunen Racing (Gear Grinders). Best run of the day, 189.379 MPH.

No. 334. No photographic trick here, the car really is that narrow.

No. 9898. Bickford Racing (SDRC). Rear Engine Streamliner, sharp and narrow.

No. 9898. Another view or, how to cheat the wind.

No. 9898. Very clean, overhead cams, transverse engine sporting a turbo which vents out the top, center.

No. 65. Earl Wooden (Sidewinders). A Crosly, stretched a little. This car and driver have been around for years and are very good at what they do.

No. 65. On race day he managed a 228.257 MPH run.

In the shaded inspection area, yes, I believe that's the Famous Mary West of the USFRA on the left. (Utah Salt Flats Racing Association, Bonneville!)

No. 557. More on this car later. Note the spoiler under the chin or nose to counteract the turbulence created by the ground effect under the car.

No. 292. The Tones (SDRC). Well shaded inspectors hard at work to ensure driver safety.

No. 292. GMC inline six, stretched wheel base, interesting air box.
Note traditional hairpin for front axle support.

Record Keeping, Classifications, someone has to do it.

No. 1120. Pigasus Racing Team, "If Pigs Could Fly." Opened up for
the inspectors. The T-shirt reads "My killer mouse only eats Fords,
Mopars and an occasional Rat."

No. 1120. Sharp entry and wind piercing fenders.

No. 1120. Fender skirts and clean exit shape, two parachutes and a vertical
stabilizer with spoiler.

No. 437. Grandpa's Merc (Sidewinders). This flathead powered Merc managed a run of 100.629 MPH. Full fendered and forty-nine at the time.

Trailer Bound. Never did get the number of this car. Note ballast in frame
rear and combination independent rear and straight front axle, skinny fronts.

No. 456. Johnston GMC (Super Fours). Off the trailer it ran 154.910 MPH.

No. 456. From this view it is Classic Track style which hasn't changed much in 40 years.

No. 456. Four exhaust headers, six injectors on a Parker manifold,
BeeJay head and interesting air box.

No. 456. Taken from slightly left of the drivers view, note chute release.

No. 357. Barbee Boy's (Super Fours). Nice '20s Roadster,
good reflection in the Moon cap. Ran 166.378 MPH.

No. 756. Shyster (Gear Grinders). A Lakester by any definition.

No. 756. Injected, blown big block, 229.139 MPH, top speed of the meet.

No. 756. What the driver sees if he looks down.

No. 216. Tom Thumb Special (Gear Grinders). Look closely at the front of this car: the axle/wheel track has been radically narrowed to cheat the wind.

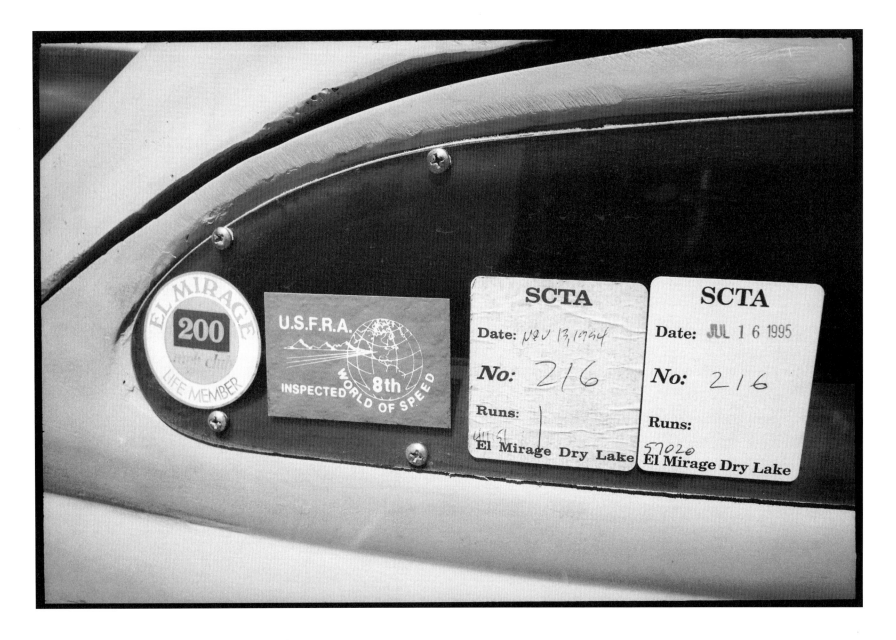

No. 216. Window detail, a '34 Ford three window coupe. It ran 201.743 MPH.

No. 414. Is getting there really half the fun?

No. 414. Wheel Center/Team iii, Wheels Liner (Gear Grinders).

No. 414. Finally off the trailer, a real attention getter.

No. 414. At last a look at the whole car, the two gents help show the size.

No. 414. Opened up for inspection. A lot of opinions were expressed. . .

No. 414. Attention to detail that is hard not to appreciate.

No. 414. It was referred to as a "liner," to me it read "Extreme Liner."

No. 414. Most spectators seemed to show a quiet admiration for the builders' skills.

No. 414. It ran, but only for a conservative test of the arrangement, 107.919 MPH. Next stop, the Bonneville Salt Flats.

The Lunch Wagon. Simply the best food and water I ever tasted. I will
never refer to one of these rigs as anything but "Lunch Wagon" ever again.

No. 130. Starbangled Banger (Super Fours).
It ran 227.542 MPH, a new record.

No. 941. Turner & Whiteley (Sidewinders). This Studebaker Truck ran 147.733 MPH for a record.

Missed the Name/Number on this car,
gives a good look at its layout.

No. 871. Dad's Dream, (Sidewinders). A Classic Model A Roadster on a
Deuce frame, Deuce grille shell.

No. 871. Full House Flathead, right side.

No. 871. Full House Flathead, left side.

No. 871. Again, family values.

No. 481. Kinkennon & Ranger, note carpeted service area.

No. 295. Dale Martin (Sidewinders).
A Triumph, possibly a 200cc. Tiger Cub.

No. 338. Ken Ohrt (Rod Riders). This is Art, (as in) less is more. . .

No. 338. The days run was 140.866 MPH.

A well-known Hot Rod Roadster on both coasts.

An Ardun conversion, blower, two Strombergs. . .
the hot set up for a flathead in any era.

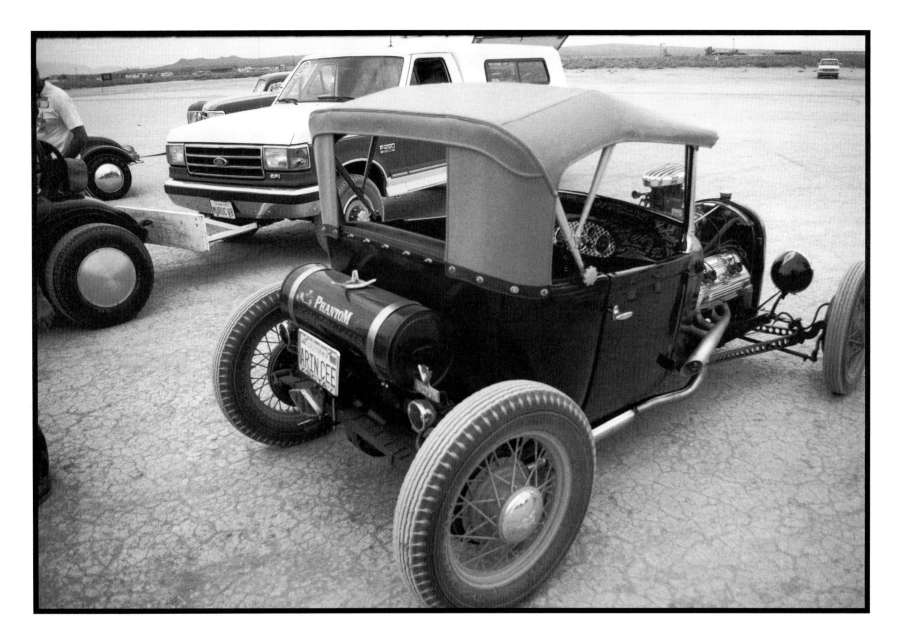

Modeled on the early Lakes Racers, ARINCEE looks right at home on the Lake.

No. 694. Salzberg, Poplawski, Noice (Sidewinders).
Does this "Look" like 149.144 MPH? It was!

No. 557. Burt and Bob Giovanine (Sidewinders). Some lessons here on
what a Roadster should be . . .

No. 557. Track nose, hot four cylinder and a lot of history here.

No. 557. Looked up Giovanine in *Throttle Magazine*, 1941 season, he ran
fours back then, a member of Albata and a winner.

No. 557. Clean and fast, 129.839 MPH.

No. 572. Monroe/Churchill/Block (Rod Riders). Along with the Camaro
(it ran 159.752 MPH) you get a scenic overview of the Lake.

No. 755. Brant-Wright Racing (Gear Grinders). Powered by an English transverse mounted motorcycle engine. Their first time out.

No. 800. Wild Bunch Racing (LSR). Studebaker on arrival at the lake.

No 800. The editorial on the roof is almost as good as the car.

No. 737. Marshall, Thayer, Glen & Banta, look closely and you can see the Hemi has just fired . . . also neat remote starter.

No. 51. Sommers-Haas Bros Spl. (Eliminators).
Yes, this image looks a little soft . . . the focus was affected by the car engine
being run up, note gent's posture in driver's seat.

My all time favorite, this car says it all for then and now. . .

Pre-Race driver meeting. They sing the National Anthem and then begin the proceedings.

Great anticipation, waiting in line to run on Race Day.

The Starting line has a great institution called Bob Higbee. No one leaves for a run without a yank on the seat belts and Bob's OK. He has been doing this for years.

One last look as the car disappears in a trail of
lake dust. Will this be a record run?

6 SUGGESTED READING

There is so much good reading material available it is difficult to know where to start. This list is based on a place to start reading on hot rods and photography and does not mean that titles or the work of others not listed are anything more than that, not listed.

From here you can start your own reading. Develop your own ideas for what you feel is good. The two subjects in this work contain what I feel is the best as introductory and basic.

Hot Rods and Their Origins

The American Hot Rod, by Dean Batchelor

Flat out, by Albert Drake

When the Hot Rods Ran, May 15, 1938. by William Carroll

Books by Don Montgomery

Authentic Hot Rods, The real good Old Days.

Hot Rod Memories Re-Lived

Hot Rods as they Were (out of Print)

Hot Rods in the 40's, Blast from the past

Continued

Photographers' Work
(well worth looking into as an
introduction)

America & Lewis Hine, Published by Aperture

Walker Evans, by James R. Mellow

Unclassified, A Walker Evans Anthology, Jeff L.
Rosenheim & Douglas Eklund

Eisenstaedt, Remembrances,
Published by Bulfinch

Eisenstaedt on Eisenstaedt,
Published by Abbeville

Imogen Cunningham,
Anything published on her works.

Margaret Bourke-White Photographer,
by Sean Callahan, Bulfinch

Robert Cappa, Published by Aperture

Robert Frank, National Gallery of Art. Scalo.

Elliott Erwitt, Published by Phaidon

Sebastiao Salgado, WORKERS,
Published by Aperture

7 SOUTHERN CALIFORNIA TIMING ASSOCIATION, INC. RESULTS SCTA DRY LAKES MEET

July 16, 1995

El Mirage, California (1.3 Mile Course)

Class and Record	Entry No.	Entry Name	Speed	Club	Points
J/BFS RECORD 168.095	555	Estrine & Vesco	151.912	SDRC	180
	9898	Bickford Racing	146.317	SDRC	174
B/FS RECORD 233.216	1120	Pigasus Racing	166.439	Eliminators	142
B/BGS RECORD					
230.000 Minimum	756	Shyster	229.139	Gear Grinders	199
C/BGS RECORD 233.254	3	Smith-Margaretich	203.813	Gear Grinders	174
AA/GS RECORD					
220.000 Minimum	414	Wheel Center/Team III Wheels Liner	107.919	Gear Grinders	98
F/BFL RECORD					
200.00 Minimum	130	Star Spangled Banger	227.542	Super Fours	252
GBFL RECORD 192.391	185	John Bjorkman	N.T.	Gear Grinders	0
J/FL RECORD 140.515	9999	Rice-Vigeant-McCabe	129.532	Gear Grinders	184

Class and Record		Entry No.	Entry Name	Speed	Club	Points
K/FL RECORD	141.259	755	Brant-Wright Racing	105.714	Gear Grinders	149
A/GL RECORD	233.313	51	Summers-Haas Bros Spl	206.408	Eliminators	184
C/GL RECORD	210.592	334	Clem-Hiltunen Racing	189.379	Gear Grinders	179
F/GL RECORD	172.040	834	Eyres, Pribyl, Sabel	158.814	SDRC	184
G/GL RECORD	158.786	98	Dave Martin	139.371	Super Fours	175
H/GL RECORD	154.462	714	Steppin' Out	172.656	Sidewinders	243
V4/FMR RECORD	164.233	557	Burt and Bob Giovanine	129.839	Sidewinders	158
C/BGMR RECORD						
210.000 Minimum		911	Fairly Honest Racing	187.455	Eliminators	178
C/GMR RECORD	201.027	262	Dad Miller Special	182.937	Road Runners	182
		34	Benham & Hope	175.529	Sidewinders	174
XF/GMR RECORD	148.464	64	Kelly & Hall Racing	143.246	Eliminators	192
		108	Brent & Brent	131.579	SDRC	177
		808	"The Eight Ball"	127.694	Eliminators	172
C/FR RECORD	205.246	811	Mammoth Automotive	170.313	Eliminators	165
H/FR RECORD						
130.000 Minimum		1203	Callaway/Doehrer	119.382	Super Fours	183
XF/BGR RECORD						
155.000 Minimum		871	Dad's Dream	117.158	Sidewinders	151
C/GR RECORD	198.677	145	Chuck Vahocick	171.402	Eliminators	172
		882	PM Automotive	158.730	Gold CstRdst	159
D/GR RECORD	197.448	369	Wilson & Waters	196.425	Super Fours	198
		1169	Mike & Bill Ferguson	162.463	Road Runners	164
		694	Salzberg, Poplawski, Nioice	149.144	Sidewinders	151
		368	Road Runner Racing	118.634	Eliminators	120

Class and Record	Entry No.	Entry Name	Speed	Club	Points
E/GR RECORD 174.410	119	Horn Special	115.969	Super Fours	132
F/GR RECORD 149.772	831	Eyres, Wavra and Finley	148.277	SDRC	198
XO/GR RECORD 154.905	28	Tom's Muffler-Deming	141.331	Rod Riders	182
	292	The Tones	140.197	SDRC	181
AA/BSTR RECORD					
200.000 Minimum	74	Noice & Confel	158.959	Sidewinders	158
D/STR RECORD 175.267	357	Barbee Boy's	166.378	Super Fours	189
E/STR RECORD 161.370	731	Bad "A"	156.671	Milers	194
V4/STR RECORD 143.540	4004	4 Ever 4	99.856	Super Fours	139
D/BFCC RECORD 224.440	737	Marshall, Thayer, Glenn & Banta	88.534	Rod Riders	78
XF/VBFCC RECORD					
155.000 Minimum	26	Tom's Muffler-Deming	157.417	Rod Riders	227
B/FCC RECORD 233.305	65	Earl Wooden	228.257	Sidewinders	195
D/FCC RECORD 204.081	216	Tom Thumb Special	201.743	Gear Grinders	197
	722	No Problem Racing	153.409	Rod Riders	150
AA/GCC RECORD					
210.000 Minimum	868	Heavy Metal Lincoln	128.001	Sidewinders	121
C/GCC RECORD 200.099	220	Lee Clancey	71.857	Sidewinders	71
H/GCC RECORD 130.057	57	Larrys Old Volks Home	88.490	Sidewinders	136
AA/FALT RECORD 209.960	689	Pretty Woman	N.T.	LSR	0
XF/BFALT RECORD					
160.000 Minimum	150	McCain & Houtz	144.967	Super Fours	181
A/FALT RECORD 212.491	598	Halopoff & Cook	173.698	LSR	163
A/BGALT RECORD 202.839	82	Snyder's Salty 'Cuda	195.483	Lakers	192

Class and Record		Entry No.	Entry Name	Speed	Club	Points
G/BGALT RECORD						
150.000 Minimum		1919	Rebel Engine	146.713	Sidewinders	195
B/GALT RECORD	202.025	363	LaBine & Rowe	191.893	Lakers	189
C/GALT RECORD	200.000	672	Hodges Bros Racing	180.257	LSR	180
		800	Wild Bunch Racing	170.766	LSR	170
		844	The Whale	164.024	Road Runners	164
E/GALT RECORD	176.125	407	Jucewic/Duncan LUV Truck	177.893	Sidewinders	226
XO/GALT RECORD	155.368	284	Farrell-Mnoian-Wolfson	106.550	Lakers	137
XO/VGALT RECORD	162.412	285	BMR Racing	159.613	Milers	196
A/BGC RECORD	196.886	304	Johnson DRM	179.127	Sidewinders	181
C/BGC RECORD	200.445	317	David Parks	76.085	Lakers	75
AA/GC RECORD	206.611	572	Monroe/Churchill/Block	159.752	Rod Riders	154
A/GC RECORD	203.473	85	Clayton & Adams	196.969	Road Runners	193
		1035	Thyer-Heathcoat-Hill	151.232	Rod Riders	148
		728	B & J Racing	140.477	Rod Riders	138
B/GC RECORD	202.025	479	Patty Wagon	163.669	Road Runners	162
D/GC RECORD	187.856	435	Sims	166.066	Road Runners	176
G/GC RECORD	146.413	380	Bob Stahl Racing	127.035	Gear Grinders	173
XF/VGC RECORD	126.057	537	Red Coupe	108.614	Sidewinders	172
		437	Granpa's Merc	100.629	Sidewinders	159
XO/VGC RECORD	139.125	256	Keith Young	131.479	Sidewinders	189
		193	Skinner & Price	124.813	SDRC	179
A/MP RECORD						
145.000 Minimum		941	Turner, Whiteley	147.733	Sidewinders	227
B/MP RECORD	142.630	164	Al Sanderson	64.634	Rod Riders	90

Class and Record		Entry No.	Entry Name	Speed	Club	Points
D/MP RECORD	167.680	166	Spirit of Havasu	131.380	Milers	158
E/MS RECORD	171.493	406	Bob Arner	133.679	Super Fours	155
C/PRO RECORD	194.258	126	Ron & Robs Monza	178.330	Sidewinders	183
		270	Duncan & Delcourts Brick	157.791	Rod Riders	162
		725	Don Ferguson Sr, Jr, III, Randy	114.849	Rod Riders	118
E/PRO RECORD	163.040	2004	Steve Clancey	106.504	Sidewinders	130
G/PRO RECORD	137.976	161	Luds Cosworth Vega	123.033	Super Fours	178
XO/PRO RECORD	130.473	266	Harold Gino	120.205	Milers	184
A/GT RECORD	193.427	27	Jeffries & SanChez	188.498	SDRC	194
E/GT RECORD	172.943	212	Wild Hair Racing	130.124	Eliminators	150
F/GT RECORD	155.105	807	Steve's Machine	156.875	Milers	226
H/GT RECORD	131.770	97	Johnston SAAB	99.461	Sidewinders	150
A/PP RECORD	139.889	691	The Old Dodge Truck	105.836	Gear Grinders	151
D/PP RECORD	121.594	832	Eyres, Simonis, Leas	82.473	SDRC	135
XO/VOT RECORD	157.754	456	Johnston GMC	154.910	Super Fours	196
TIME ONLY		662	End of Trail	T.O.	Eliminators	0

MOTORCYCLES

Class and Record		Entry No.	Entry Name	Speed	Club	Points
C/SFM RECORD	199.867	830	Nick Larson	90.105	Sidewinders	90
H/SFM RECORD	163.517	497	Mike Burns/Yamaha 250	135.413	Sidewinders	165
L/SFM RECORD						
75.000 Minimum		576	Cummings & Strahm III	75.153	Gear Grinders	225
D/FM RECORD						
170.000 Minimum		481	Kinkennon and Ranger	N.S.	SDRC	0

Class and Record		Entry No.	Entry Name	Speed	Club	Points
E/FM RECORD	168.350	11	David Dastrup/Twist-Off Racing	164.543	SDRC	195
F/VFM RECORD	118.368	5	Tatro Machine Special	118.567	SDRC	225
G/FM RECORD	146.771	10	David Willis	141.420	Rod Riders	192
H/FM RECORD	139.555	495	Mike Burns/Yamaha 250	43.323	Sidewinders	62
K/FM RECORD						
90.000 Minimum		415	Cummings and Strahm II	84.206	Gear Grinders	187
A/SGM RECORD	202.383	70	Matt Capri- South Bay Triumph	140.714	SDRC	139
B/SGM RECORD	206.100	328	Dr. Suda ZZ-R	176.516	Sidewinders	171
C/SGM RECORD						
190.000 Minimum		168	South Bay Triumph – Mike Emmings	N.T.	Sidewinders	0
F/SGM RECORD	166.970	869	Dads Ride	77.365	Gear Grinders	92
H/SGM RECORD	155.145	498	Mike Burns/Yamaha 250	140.451	Sidewinders	181
L/SGM RECORD						
70.000 Minimum		575	Cummings and Strahm I	72.185	Gear Grinders	227
B/GM RECORD	196.326	340	Don Watkins-Team Dingus	169.330	Eliminators	172
C/GM RECORD	156.985	231	McKibben Engineering Co.	156.985	Gear Grinders	189
		611	Ron Cook/Sims & Rohm	156.006	Sidewinders	187
D/VGM RECORD	116.392	4	Full House Mouse	114.489	SDRC	196
E/VGM RECORD		290	Terry Lewis	107.740	SDRC	178
/GM RECORD	155.790	272	Erlenbach Racing	139.162	Gear Grinders	178
		803	Wild Bunch Racing	109.720	LSR	140
G/GM RECORD	148.870	171	Gary Niemetschek	T.O.	Rod Riders	0
H/GM RECORD	137.544	1123	Mail-Order America	139.708	Gear Grinders	227
B/PFM RECORD	172.140	127	Winks Lakester	106.893	Gear Grinders	124
C/PFM RECORD	146.480	338	Ken Ohrt	140.866	Rod Riders	192

Class and Record			Entry No.	Entry Name	Speed	Club	Points
A/PGM RECORD	161.899		271	Keith Kardell/Bartel's H-D	141.726	Sidewinders	175
			660	Greenleaf	90.670	Gear Grinders	112
H/PGM RECORD	90.929		295	Dale Martin	86.497	Sidewinders	190

TOP SPEED OF MEET (CAR) – B/BGS – Shyster – 229.139 MPH

TOP SPEED OF MEET (MOTORCYCLE) – B/SGM – Dr. Suda ZZ-R – 176.516 MPH

MORE TITLES FROM ICONOGRAFIX:

All Iconografix books are available from direct mail specialty book dealers and bookstores worldwide, or can be ordered from the publisher. For book trade and distribution information or to add your name to our mailing list and receive a **FREE CATALOG** contact:

Iconografix, PO Box 446, Hudson, Wisconsin, 54016   Telephone: (715) 381-9755, (800) 289-3504 (USA), Fax: (715) 381-9756

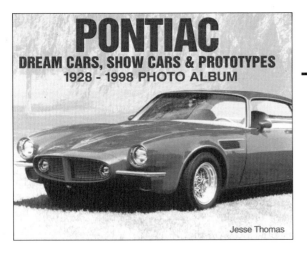
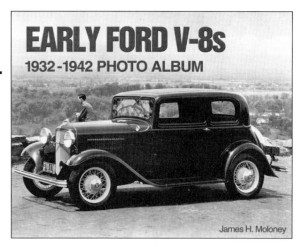

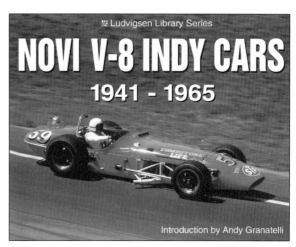
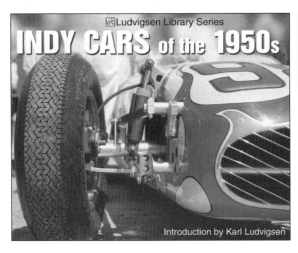
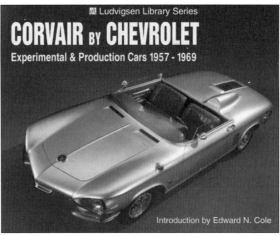
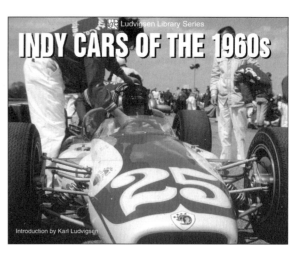